Fill in your passport. Don't forget to draw your picture!

MORE FUN WITH ENGLISH

Address _____

_____

_____

_____

_____

Eye colour _____

Name _____ Hair colour _____

Height _____

_____

Age _____ Weight _____

by **Kay Hiatt**

designed and illustrated by **Claire James**

Ladybird Books

THE ALPHABET

Check that you know your alphabet.
Join the dots in alphabetical order to complete the picture below.

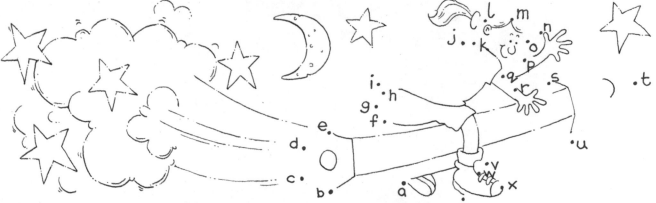

Write the alphabet again using capital letters.

A

Libraries and bookshops often arrange their books by putting the authors' second names in alphabetical order.

Put these books in order.

A Guide to Houseplants by Ivy Leaf ☐
Waterfalls of the World by C. Rivers ☐
The Great Escape by Digger Tunnel ☐
Beginning Astronomy by I. C. Stars ☐
Going Camping by Ivor Tent ☐
Making Cakes by R. U. Hungry ☐1

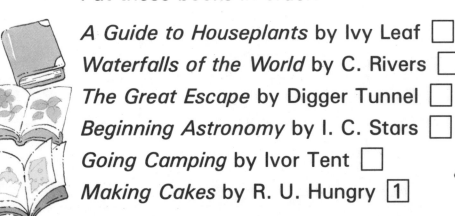

In which order are these words in the dictionary?

☐ **spider**
☐ **penguin**
☐ **seal**
☐ **fox**
☐ **parrot**
☐1 **fish**
☐ **lion**
☐ **leopard**

When two words sta
with the same letter
look at the second let
If that is the same, lo
at the third and so o

NOUNS

Proper nouns are

names of people:
names of places:
days of the week:
months of the year:

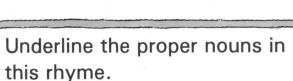

Simon Claire
Paris France
Monday Friday
February June

Proper nouns always begin with a capital letter.

Underline the proper nouns in this rhyme.

Thirty days have September,
April, June and November.
All the rest have thirty one,
except February alone,
which has twenty eight days clear
and twenty nine in each leap year.

Do you know when the next leap year is?

Fill in your passport. Remember the capital letters.

The day you were born...

Your name...

The country where you were born....

The town where you were born...

Common nouns have a capital letter only at the *beginning of a sentence.*

Put each of these common nouns in the correct box.

Things I use in the kitchen	Things I use in the garden

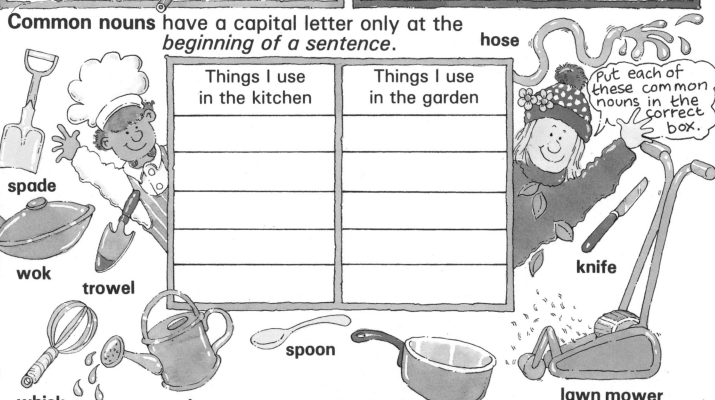

spade

wok

trowel

whisk

watering can

spoon

saucepan

hose

knife

lawn mower

SENTENCES MAKE SENSE

A sentence starts with a capital letter and ends with a full stop.

The capital letters and full stops help to make sense of a piece of writing. Sentences make sense.

Write each of these sentences underneath the correct picture.

Plant cress seeds on top.

Fill it with damp soil.

Draw a face on a clean empty eggshell.

The cress will soon grow.

1 _ _ _ _ _ _ _ _ _ _ _ _ _ _ _ _ 2 _ _ _ _ _ _ _ _ _ _ _ _ _

3 _ _ _ _ _ _ _ _ _ _ _ _ _ _ _ _ 4 _ _ _ _ _ _ _ _ _ _ _ _

The capital letters and full stops are missing from this piece. Can you put them in?

i made a calendar at school first i took a paper plate and drew a picture on it next i made two holes in the top and put a piece of string through them to make a loop i stuck a calendar on the bottom my mum really liked it

Did you find 5 sentences?

NOUNS, ADJECTIVES, VERBS

We need nouns, adjectives and verbs in our speech and writing.

Remember
- nouns *name* things.
- adjectives *describe* things.
- verbs *do* things.

Find them in the word search below

Nouns
rocket
planet
monster
astronaut

Adjectives
cold
fast
windy
green

Verbs
ran
chased
escaped
flew

c	d	g	e	q	g	f	l	e	w
h	j	r	k	a	p	q	r	s	t
a	u	e	e	s	c	a	p	e	d
s	v	e	w	t	w	i	n	d	y
e	x	n	z	r	o	c	k	e	t
d	b	w	c	o	l	d	d	f	g
h	p	l	a	n	e	t	j	k	l
m	n	r	f	a	s	t	p	q	r
s	v	a	w	u	x	z	y	b	d
m	o	n	s	t	e	r	g	c	f

Use these words to complete this story.

It was the year 3000 and my a_____ friend

and I f_____ to a distant p_____ in my r_____.

It was a c_____ and w_____ planet. A g_____

m_____ saw us and c_____ us. We r___ as f_____

as we could and e_____ to our rocket. The monster

ran faster than us. He said he only wanted to say hello!

ADJECTIVES CAN CHANGE

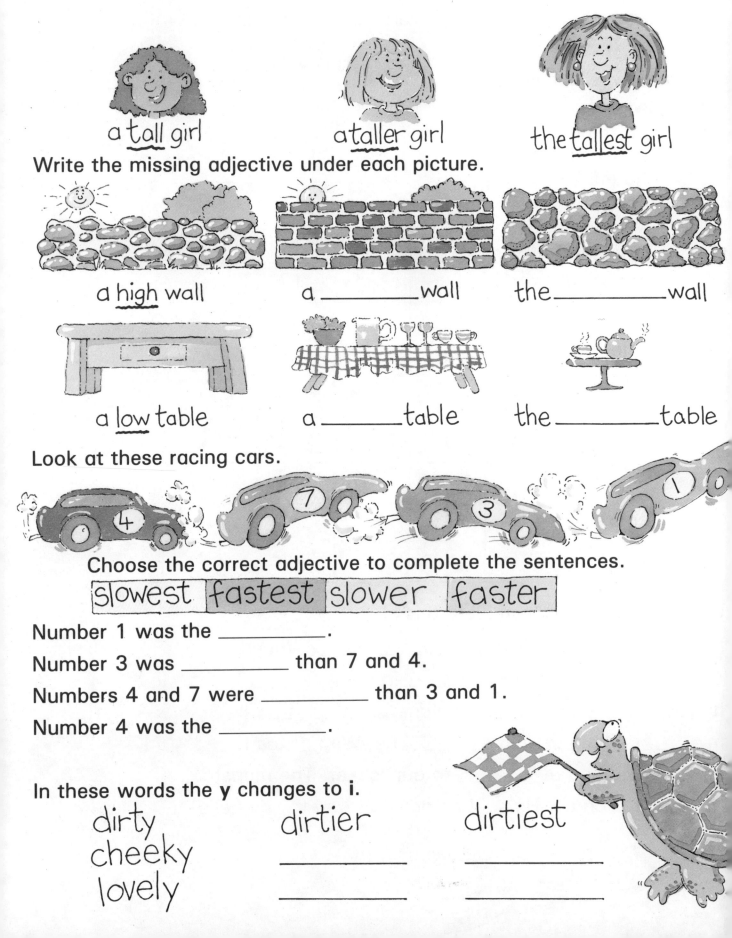

a <u>tall</u> girl   a <u>taller</u> girl   the <u>tallest</u> girl

Write the missing adjective under each picture.

a <u>high</u> wall   a _____ wall   the _____ wall

a <u>low</u> table   a _____ table   the _____ table

Look at these racing cars.

Choose the correct adjective to complete the sentences.

| slowest | fastest | slower | faster |

Number 1 was the _____ .

Number 3 was _____ than 7 and 4.

Numbers 4 and 7 were _____ than 3 and 1.

Number 4 was the _____ .

In these words the **y** changes to **i**.

dirty   dirtier   dirtiest

cheeky   _____   _____

lovely   _____   _____

QUESTIONS AND ANSWERS

Questions start with a capital letter and end with a question mark.
Match each question to the answer.

What is your name?

Where do you live?

How old are you?

I live on Planet Zuk.

My name is Zukon.

I am 2000 years old.

This boy saw a bank robbery.
The detective asked a lot of questions.
What do you think he asked?

Draw a picture of the robber.

Q _____
_____

A He was very tall.

Q _____
_____

A He was wearing a black coat
and a black mask.

Q _____
_____

A He had yellow trainers.

SPELLING SUCCESS

LOOK	SAY	COVER	WRITE	CHECK
at the word.	the word.	the word.	the word.	the word.

Try these:

work _____ ☐   pork _____ ☐

fork _____ ☐   cork _____ ☐

Use the words to finish these sentences.

1 All _____ and no play makes Jack a dull boy.

2 A wine bottle has a _____ in its neck.

3 A baby can't use a knife and _____.

4 He loved roast _____ with apple sauce.

Did you get them right?

RULE – Drop the e when adding ing

write		**writing**
drive		**driving**
wave		**waving**
skate		**skating**

e

Now try these:

dance _____

dive _____

hide _____

ride _____

Put the words in the right places.

writing   driving

waving

skating

_____ _____ a letter

_____ _____ a car

_____ _____ to a friend

_____ _____ on thin ice

Make up sentences of your own using your new **ing** words.

WORD DETECTIVE

Longer words sometimes have short words hidden inside them.
Read these:

our red ant we hat me so be use the

Now find them again in these words and draw a circle round them.

they   some   what

four   want

tired   because   were

Practise spelling these words.

LOOK	SAY	COVER	WRITE	CHECK

How many ticks?

_____ ☐   _____ ☐
_____ ☐   _____ ☐
_____ ☐   _____ ☐
_____ ☐   _____ ☐

Find the word **arm** inside the words on the bees.

warm   harm   farm

alarm   armour   army

What do you call lots of bees?

A _____

Write the words again.

_ _

PREFIXES AND SUFFIXES

Adding small groups of letters to the beginning or end of a word can change its meaning.

Letters added at the beginning are called **prefixes**.

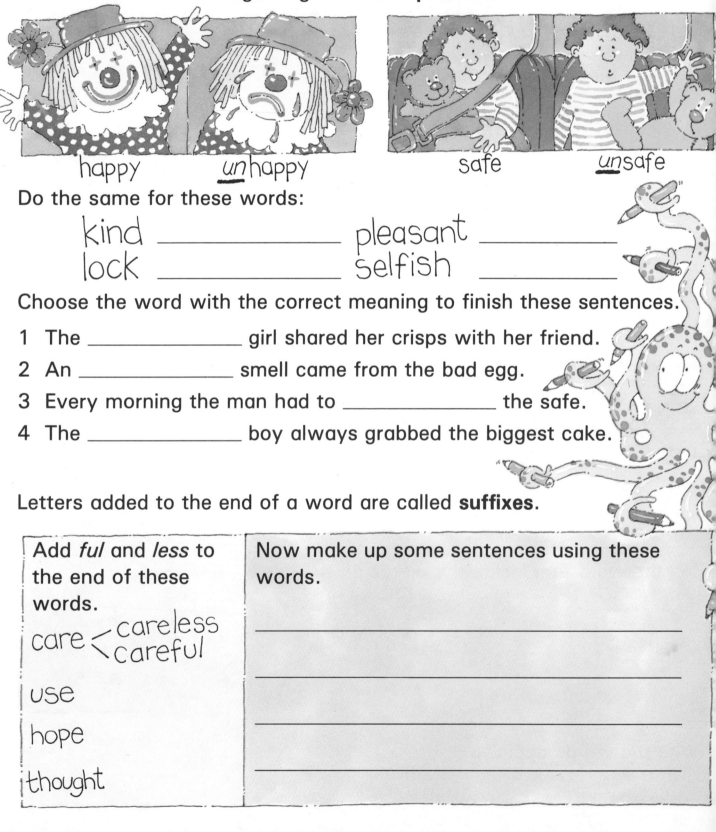

happy   unhappy   safe   unsafe

Do the same for these words:

kind _____   pleasant _____
lock _____   selfish _____

Choose the word with the correct meaning to finish these sentences.

1 The _____ girl shared her crisps with her friend.

2 An _____ smell came from the bad egg.

3 Every morning the man had to _____ the safe.

4 The _____ boy always grabbed the biggest cake.

Letters added to the end of a word are called **suffixes**.

Add *ful* and *less* to the end of these words.	Now make up some sentences using these words.
care < careless / careful	_____
use	_____
hope	_____
thought	_____

SOUNDS THE SAME

Some words have an **f** sound when we say them but this sound
is spelt **ph** when we write the word.

Work out the answers to these clues and fill in the blanks below.

1 There are 26 letters in this.   1 __ph_____

2 You need a camera to take one of these.   2 ph_____ph

3 Use this to speak to someone in
   another town.   3 _____ph____

4 This animal is a great swimmer.   4 ____ph__

5 Large grey animal with a trunk.   5 ____ph____

Sometimes a c sounds like s.
Fill in the missing c in this story.

____inderella wanted to go to

the ball. She got lost in the ____ity

____entre and went to the ____ircus

instead. A juggling ____entipede called

for a coach and ____inderella

finally reached the ball.

LOOK   SAY   COVER   WRITE   CHECK

Write out all the **c** words again.

_____

_____

HOMONYMS

Homonyms are words which *sound* the same and are sometimes spelt the same but which have **different** meanings.

For example:

bat | bat | leek | leak

Choose the correct word to complete these sentences.

1 The woman bought some half price shoes in the _____ (**sail, sale**).

2 The man went to a barber to have his _____ (**hair, hare**) cut.

3 The _____ (**son, sun**) came out from behind a cloud.

4 The children built a sandcastle on the _____ (**beech, beach**).

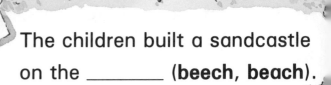

Do you know the meaning of all the other words?

5 The _____ (**knight, night**) wore a heavy suit of armour.

6 The dog wagged its _____ (**tail, tale**).

INSTRUCTIONS AND IDEAS FOR GAMES TO PLAY USING THE CARD WHICH FOLLOWS ARE PRINTED ON THE INSIDE BACK COVER.

SYNONYMS

Synonyms are different words which have nearly the same meaning.

For example:

huge/enormous

dirty/unclean

Match these words to their synonyms.

Use a dictionary to help you.

courage   hard   copy   adore   rapid

coarse   faithful   forgive

bravery _____   love _____

quick _____   loyal _____

difficult _____   reproduce _____

rough _____   pardon _____

Read these sentences and write a synonym for the word shown in bold letters.

1 I **like** this book. _____

2 The **big** dog was like a small pony. _____

3 The boss was **angry** when Tom was late. _____

4 The **little** girl couldn't reach the shelf. _____

LETTER PATTERNS

Look out for groups of letters inside words.

Fill in the missing **dge** pattern in these instructions and help Goldilocks to find the porridge.

Walk along the path at the e_____ of the wood.

Cross over the bri_____ and go past the tall he_____.

Do_____ between the beehives.

Look for the porri_____ on the le_____ with the honey on it.

Now find the words again in this word search.

a	b	c	l	e	d	g	e
a	h	e	d	g	e	f	d
c	d	l	m	n	o	p	g
p	o	r	r	i	d	g	e
q	d	s	t	u	v	w	x
b	g	b	r	i	d	g	e
a	e	c	d	e	f	h	i

Can you spot the **eo** pattern?
Draw a circle round it then cover the words and write them again.

people _____

leotard _____

leopard _____

pigeon _____

Remember there's a pig inside a pigeon!

MORE LETTER PATTERNS

Draw a circle round the **ough** pattern in these words.

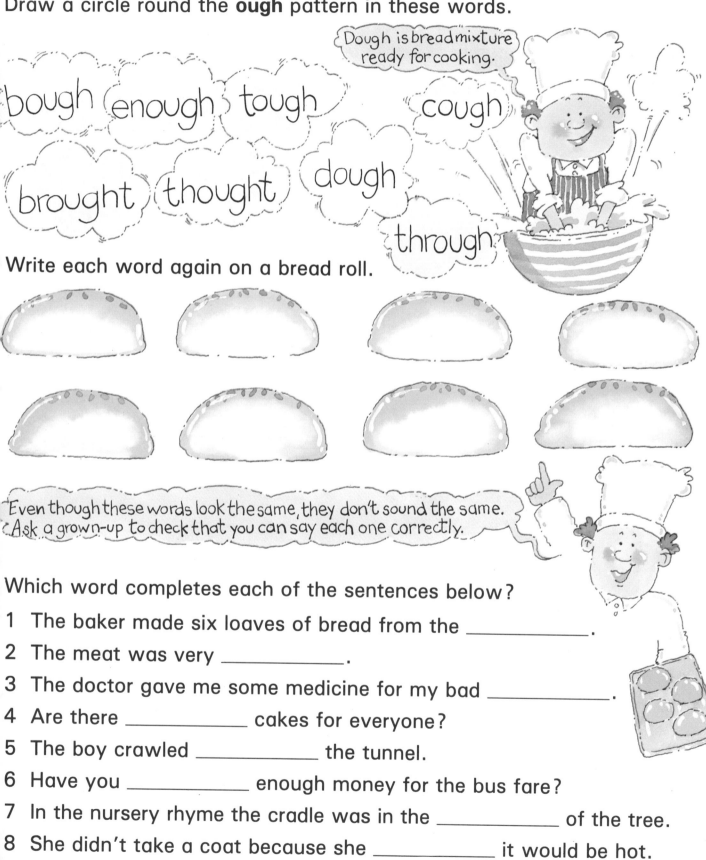

Dough is bread mixture ready for cooking.

bough enough tough cough

brought thought dough

through

Write each word again on a bread roll.

Even though these words look the same, they don't sound the same. Ask a grown-up to check that you can say each one correctly.

Which word completes each of the sentences below?

1 The baker made six loaves of bread from the _____.

2 The meat was very _____.

3 The doctor gave me some medicine for my bad _____.

4 Are there _____ cakes for everyone?

5 The boy crawled _____ the tunnel.

6 Have you _____ enough money for the bus fare?

7 In the nursery rhyme the cradle was in the _____ of the tree.

8 She didn't take a coat because she _____ it would be hot.

SAYINGS

Some sayings don't mean exactly what they say.

She was full of beans means that she was **energetic and lively** not that she was actually *full of beans*.

Tick the real meaning of these sayings.

When Tom's cat died it broke his heart.

1 Tom's heart fell to pieces. ☐
2 Tom was very sad and upset. ☐

My mum was over the moon.

1 She was very, very pleased. ☐
2 She was flying over the moon. ☐

My brother was down in the dumps.

1 He was walking round a rubbish dump. ☐
2 He was feeling unhappy. ☐

Write a sentence to describe the
real meaning of these sayings.

He was a wet blanket.

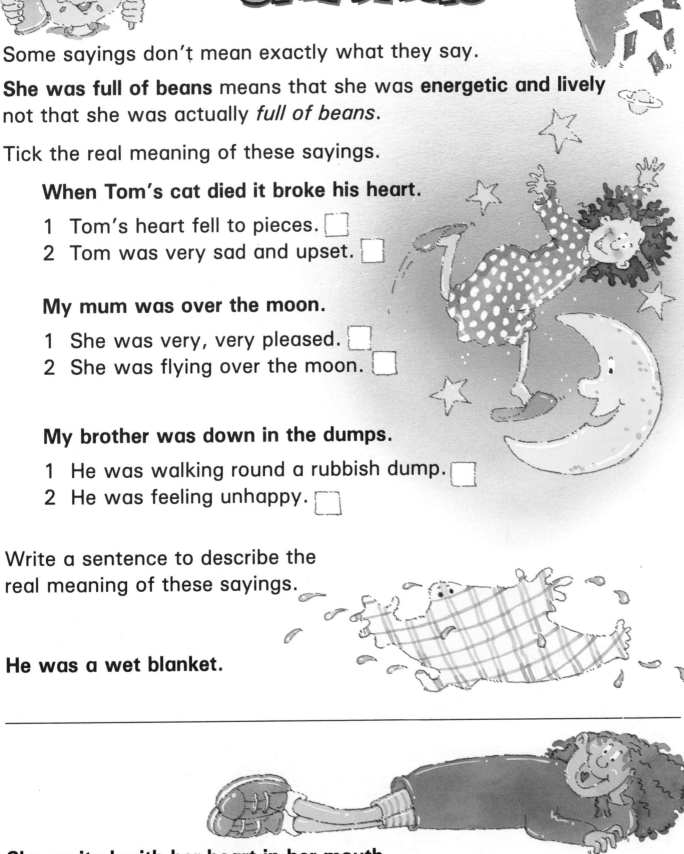

She waited with her heart in her mouth.

SIMILES

A **simile** (say *simily*) describes something by making it like something else.

Similes usually have **as** or **like** in the description.

a s   l i k e

The baby was **as good as gold** means she was very well behaved.

Complete these similes:

ice

feather

iron

as fierce as a _____

as light as a _____

as hard as _____

as wise as an _____

as green as _____

as cold as _____

grass

owl

lion

Complete these similes:

as strong as _____

as quiet as _____

as quick as _____

as slow as _____

ADJECTIVES ADD SPICE

Using **adjectives** to describe nouns can make your writing much more interesting and exciting.

Look at all the vegetables in this delicious soup and draw a line to the adjective that you think makes each vegetable sound more interesting.

onions	crunchy
carrots	chunky
leeks	green
potatoes	chopped
turnips	golden
beans	fresh
peas	tasty
parsnip	diced

Write out your list of vegetables again with their adjectives.

_____

_____

_____

_____

_____

_____

_____

Make up a dinner menu for a hungry giant. Use lots of adjectives to describe each dish.

STOP USING NICE

One adjective which is often used too much is **nice**.
It can be very boring!

Count how many times the word nice is used in the story below.

Karl was a nice boy. He lived in a nice house. He had a nice Mum and a nice Dad and his dog was nice too. He always wore nice clothes. On his birthday he was given a nice bike.

How many times? ☐

Read the adjectives below.

friendly, little, big, jolly, crazy, generous, noisy, colourful, scruffy, smart, new, terrific.

Choose from the list or add your own and write the story again *without using the word* **nice**.

_____

_____

_____

_____

_____

_____

_____

_____

_____

_____

MORE LETTER PATTERNS

Here is an ac**tion** robot. Give him a name.

Guide the robot through this maze. As he goes past each word, underline the **tion** pattern.

invention

junction

function

question

direction

action

Write each word again using:

LOOK   SAY   COVER   WRITE   CHECK

_____   _____

_____   _____

_____

On a piece of paper, write 6 sentences using each of these words.

Look carefully at the picture of the robot and write your answer.
Either ☑ , ☒ or ?

1 He has a round head. ☐

2 He has green eyes. ☐

3 He can speak. ☐

4 He can move in all directions. ☐

5 He has large feet. ☐

TO, TWO, TOO

To, two and too all sound the same but have different meanings.
For example:

> I went to the cinema.
> My friend came too.
> I paid for the two of us.

These sentences have **to**, **too** or **two** missing. Fill in the correct word.

1 The train leaves at _____ minutes past five.

2 The boy ran _____ school.

3 The elephant was _____ big _____ get through the door.

4 She wanted _____ be an astronaut and go _____ the moon.

OF, OFF

Of and off are spelt differently and have different meanings.
For example:

> A pair of gloves.
> The plane took off.

Put either **of** or **off** in the spaces.

1 It was hot so I took _____ my coat.

2 Sam was the captain _____ the team.

3 The girl got _____ the swing so that her friend could have a turn.

4 A lot _____ people got _____ the bus.

READING BETWEEN THE LINES

Sometimes when we're reading we have to look for clues. Then, like a detective, we put the clues together in order to make sense and to understand more about what we have read.

This is called *reading between the lines*.

eg

Dad is standing by the washing machine sorting out a pile of dirty clothes. He is not smiling!

1 What is he going to do?
cook lunch ☐
do the washing ☐

2 Where is he?
in the kitchen ☐
in the bedroom ☐

3 Is he enjoying himself?
Yes ☐   No ☐

You try these.

A girl is running along the road with a bag in one hand and some money in the other hand.

1 Where is she going?
to the cinema ☐
to the shops ☐

2 What will she have to do if she wants to blow her nose?

His hands are on the steering wheel and his foot is on the brake.

1 What is he doing?
driving a car ☐
riding a bicycle ☐

2 Is he going fast? ☐
Has he stopped?
YES/NO/
DON'T KNOW

3 Is he with someone?
YES/NO/DON'T KNOW

4 Is the man excited?
YES/NO/DON'T KNOW

MISSING LETTERS

I am can be written in a short way as **I'm**.

Is not can be shortened to **isn't**.

We very often say these words in the short way when we talk to someone. The ' is called an apostrophe (say apostrofee).

An apostrophe is used in writing to show that some letters are missing.

Match the words below to their short form.

we are	wouldn't
can not	they're
they are	we're
would not	can't
it is	won't
I would	it's
will not	I'd

Now rewrite the letter below using shortened words with their apostrophe.

Dear Jane
   I would love to come and see you but I am afraid it will not be possible this week. I can not find anyone to look after my dog and it would not be fair to leave him.
I will ring when it is easier to leave him.
   Love from Tim. x

GIVE YOURSELF A TEST...

Find some paper and give yourself 20 minutes to do this test.

Use | LOOK | SAY | COVER | WRITE | CHECK | for the spelling exercises!

GOOD LUCK!

1 Put all the capital letters and full stops in the right places.

fred and his friend adam went fishing in the river rushing it was raining fred had no raincoat so adam ran back to fred's house in market street to get a coat for him

2 Write 4 common nouns and list them in alphabetical order.

3 Write 2 adjectives to go with each noun.

4 Write a question to go with each of these answers.

My birthday is in June and I shall be 10.

The man had to wait for half an hour because the train was late.

5 Spell these words.

through

working machine

bought

bridge

building

photograph

invention

6 Fill in the missing adjectives.

high _____ highest
dirty dirtier _____
_____ longer longest
pretty _____ prettiest